THE NECESSARY
ART OF PERSUASION

Harvard Business Review

CLASSICS

THE NECESSARY ART OF PERSUASION

Jay A. Conger

Harvard Business Press
Boston, Massachusetts

Library of Congress Cataloging-in-Publication Data

Conger, Jay Alden.
 The necessary art of persuasion / Jay A. Conger.
   p. cm. — (Harvard business review classics)
 ISBN 978-1-4221-2671-4
 1. Persuasion (Psychology) in organizations. 2. Communication
in management. I. Title.
 HD30.3.C6535 2008
 658.4′5—dc22

                                2008022294

The paper used in this publication meets the requirements of the
American National Standard for Permanence of Paper for Publica-
tions and Documents in Libraries and Archives Z39.48-1992.

THE
HARVARD BUSINESS REVIEW
CLASSICS SERIES

Since 1922, *Harvard Business Review* has been a leading source of breakthrough ideas in management practice—many of which still speak to and influence us today. The HBR Classics series now offers you the opportunity to make these seminal pieces a part of your permanent management library. Each volume contains a groundbreaking idea that has shaped best practices and inspired countless managers around the world—and will change how you think about the business world today.

THE NECESSARY ART
OF PERSUASION

If there ever was a time for business-people to learn the fine art of persuasion, it is now. Gone are the command-and-control days of executives managing by decree. Today businesses are run largely by cross-functional teams of peers and populated by baby boomers and their Generation X offspring, who show little tolerance for unquestioned authority. Electronic communication and globalization have further eroded the traditional hierarchy, as ideas and people flow more freely than ever around organizations and as decisions get made closer to the markets. These fundamental changes, more than a decade in the making but now firmly part of the economic landscape, essentially come down to this: work today gets done in an environment where people don't just ask What should I do? but Why should I do it?

To answer this why question effectively is to persuade. Yet many businesspeople misunderstand persuasion, and more still underutilize it. The reason? Persuasion is widely perceived as a skill reserved for selling products and closing deals. It is also commonly seen as just another form of manipulation—devious and to be avoided. Certainly, persuasion can be used in selling and deal-clinching situations, and it can be mis-used to manipulate people. But exercised constructively and to its full potential, per-suasion supersedes sales and is quite the op-posite of deception. Effective persuasion becomes a negotiating and learning process through which a persuader leads colleagues to a problem's shared solution. Persuasion does indeed involve moving people to a posi-tion they don't currently hold, but not by begging or cajoling. Instead, it involves care-ful preparation, the proper framing of argu-ments, the presentation of vivid supporting evidence, and the effort to find the correct emotional match with your audience.

Effective persuasion is a difficult and time-consuming proposition, but it may also be more powerful than the command-and-control managerial model it succeeds. As AlliedSignal's CEO Lawrence Bossidy said recently, "The day when you could yell and scream and beat people into good performance is over. Today you have to appeal to them by helping them see how they can get from here to there, by establishing some credibility, and by giving them some reason and help to get there. Do all those things, and they'll knock down doors." In essence, he is describing persuasion—now more than ever, the language of business leadership.

Think for a moment of your definition of persuasion. If you are like most business-people I have encountered (see "Twelve Years of Watching and Listening" at the end of this article), you see persuasion as a relatively straightforward process. First, you strongly state your position. Second, you outline the supporting arguments, followed by a highly assertive, data-based exposition. Finally, you enter the deal-making stage and work toward a "close." In other words, you use logic, persistence, and personal enthusiasm to get others to buy a good idea. The reality is that following this process is one surefire way to fail at persuasion. (See "Four Ways Not to Persuade" at the end of this article.)

What, then, constitutes effective persuasion? If persuasion is a learning and negotiating process, then in the most general terms it involves phases of discovery, preparation, and dialogue. Getting ready to persuade colleagues can take weeks or months of planning as you learn about your audience and the position you intend to argue. Before they even start to talk, effective persuaders have considered their positions from every angle. What investments in time and money will my position require from others? Is my supporting evidence weak in any way? Are there alternative positions I need to examine?

Dialogue happens before and during the persuasion process. Before the process begins, effective persuaders use dialogue to learn more about their audience's opinions, concerns, and perspectives. During the process, dialogue continues to be a form of learning, but it is also the beginning of the negotiation stage. You invite people to discuss, even debate, the merits of your position, and then to offer honest feedback and suggest alternative solutions. That may sound like a slow way to achieve your goal, but effective persuasion is about testing and revising ideas in concert with your colleagues' concerns and needs. In fact, the best persuaders not only listen to others but also incorporate their perspectives into a shared solution.

Persuasion, in other words, often involves –indeed, demands–compromise. Perhaps that is why the most effective persuaders seem to share a common trait: they are open-minded, never dogmatic. They enter the persuasion process prepared to adjust their viewpoints and incorporate others' ideas. That approach to persuasion is, interestingly, highly persuasive in itself. When colleagues see that a persuader is eager to hear their views and willing to make changes in response to their needs and concerns, they respond very positively. They trust the persuader more and listen more attentively. They don't fear being bowled over or manipulated. They see the persuader as flexible and are thus more willing to make sacrifices themselves. Because that is such a powerful dynamic, good persuaders often enter the persuasion process with judicious compromises already prepared.

FOUR ESSENTIAL STEPS

Effective persuasion involves four distinct and essential steps. First, effective persuaders establish credibility. Second, they frame their goals in a way that identifies common ground with those they intend to persuade. Third, they reinforce their positions using vivid language and compelling evidence. And fourth, they connect emotionally with their audience. As one of the most effective executives in our research commented, "The most valuable lesson I've learned about persuasion over the years is that there's just as much strategy in how you present your position as in the position itself. In fact, I'd say the strategy of presentation is the more critical."

Establish credibility

The first hurdle persuaders must overcome is their own credibility. A persuader can't advocate a new or contrarian position without having people wonder, Can we trust this individual's perspectives and opinions? Such a reaction is understandable. After all, allowing oneself to be persuaded is risky, because any new initiative demands a commitment of time and resources. Yet even though persuaders must have high credibility, our research strongly suggests that most managers overestimate their own credibility— considerably.

In the workplace, credibility grows out of two sources: expertise and relationships. People are considered to have high levels of expertise if they have a history of sound judgment or have proven themselves knowledgeable and well informed about their proposals. For example, in proposing a new product idea, an effective persuader would need to be perceived as possessing a thorough understanding of the product—its specifications, target markets, customers, and competing products. A history of prior successes would further strengthen the persuader's perceived expertise. One extremely successful executive in our research had a track record of 14 years of devising highly effective advertising campaigns. Not surprisingly, he had an easy time winning colleagues over to his position. Another manager had a track record of seven successful new-product launches in a period of five years. He, too, had an advantage when it came to persuading his colleagues to support his next new idea.

On the relationship side, people with high credibility have demonstrated—again, usually over time—that they can be trusted to listen and to work in the best interests of others. They have also consistently shown strong emotional character and integrity; that is, they are not known for mood extremes or inconsistent performance. Indeed, people who are known to be honest, steady, and reliable have an edge when going into any persuasion situation. Because their relationships are robust, they are more apt to be given the benefit of the doubt. One effective persuader in our research was considered by colleagues to be remarkably trustworthy and fair; many people confided in her. In addition, she generously shared credit for good ideas and provided staff with exposure to the company's senior executives. This woman had built strong relationships, which meant her staff and peers were always willing to consider seriously what she proposed.

If expertise and relationships determine credibility, it is crucial that you undertake an honest assessment of where you stand on both criteria before beginning to persuade. To do so, first step back and ask yourself the following questions related to expertise: How will others perceive my knowledge about the strategy, product, or change I am proposing? Do I have a track record in this area that others know about and respect? Then, to assess the strength of your relationship credibility, ask yourself, Do those I am hoping to persuade see me as helpful, trustworthy, and supportive? Will they see me as someone in sync with them—emotionally, intellectually, and politically—on issues like this one? Finally, it is important to note that it is not enough to get your own read on these matters. You must also test your answers with colleagues you trust to give you a reality check. Only then will you have a complete picture of your credibility.

In most cases, that exercise helps people discover that they have some measure of weakness, either on the expertise or on the relationship side of credibility. The challenge then becomes to fill in such gaps.

In general, if your area of weakness is on the expertise side, you have several options:

- First, you can learn more about the complexities of your position through either formal or informal education and through conversations with knowledgeable individuals. You might also get more relevant experience on the job by asking, for instance, to be assigned to a team that would increase your insight into particular markets or products.

- Another alternative is to hire someone to bolster your expertise—for example, an industry consultant or a recognized outside expert, such as a professor. Either one may have the knowledge and experience required to support your position effectively. Similarly, you may tap experts within your organization to advocate your position. Their credibility becomes a substitute for your own.

- You can also utilize other outside sources
  of information to support your position,
  such as respected business or trade pe-
  riodicals, books, independently produced
  reports, and lectures by experts. In our
  research, one executive from the cloth-
  ing industry successfully persuaded his
  company to reposition an entire product line to a more youthful market after
  bolstering his credibility with articles
  by a noted demographer in two highly
  regarded journals and with two independent market-research studies.

- Finally, you may launch pilot projects
  to demonstrate on a small scale your
  expertise and the value of your ideas.

As for filling in the relationship gap:

- You should make a concerted effort to meet one-on-one with all the key people you plan to persuade. This is not the time to outline your position but rather to get a range of perspectives on the issue at hand. If you have the time and resources, you should even offer to help these people with issues that concern them.

- Another option is to involve like-minded coworkers who already have strong relationships with your audience. Again, that is a matter of seeking out substitutes on your own behalf.

For an example of how these strategies can be put to work, consider the case of a chief operating officer of a large retail bank, whom we will call Tom Smith. Although he was new to his job, Smith ardently wanted to persuade the senior management team that the company was in serious trouble. He believed that the bank's overhead was excessive and would jeopardize its position as the industry entered a more competitive era. Most of his colleagues, however, did not see the potential seriousness of the situation. Because the bank had been enormously successful in recent years, they believed changes in the industry posed little danger. In addition to being newly appointed, Smith had another problem: his career had been in financial services, and he was considered an outsider in the world of retail banking. Thus he had few personal connections to draw on as he made his case, nor was he perceived to be particularly knowledgeable about marketplace exigencies.

As a first step in establishing credibility, Smith hired an external consultant with respected credentials in the industry who showed that the bank was indeed poorly positioned to be a low-cost producer. In a series of interactive presentations to the bank's top-level management, the consultant revealed how the company's leading competitors were taking aggressive actions to contain operating costs. He made it clear from these presentations that not cutting costs would soon cause the bank to fall drastically behind the competition. These findings were then distributed in written reports that circulated throughout the bank.

Next, Smith determined that the bank's branch managers were critical to his campaign. The buy-in of those respected and informed individuals would signal to others in the company that his concerns were valid. Moreover, Smith looked to the branch managers because he believed that they could increase his expertise about marketplace trends and also help him test his own assumptions. Thus, for the next three months, he visited every branch in his region of Ontario, Canada—135 in all. During each visit, he spent time with branch managers, listening to their perceptions of the bank's strengths and weaknesses. He learned first-hand about the competition's initiatives and customer trends, and he solicited ideas for improving the bank's services and minimizing costs. By the time he was through, Smith had a broad perspective on the bank's future that few people even in senior management possessed. And he had built dozens of relationships in the process.

Finally, Smith launched some small but highly visible initiatives to demonstrate his expertise and capabilities. For example, he was concerned about slow growth in the company's mortgage business and the loan officers' resulting slip in morale. So he devised a program in which new mortgage customers would make no payments for the first 90 days. The initiative proved remarkably successful, and in short order Smith appeared to be a far more savvy retail banker than anyone had assumed.

Another example of how to establish credibility comes from Microsoft. In 1990, two product-development managers, Karen Fries and Barry Linnett, came to believe that the market would greatly welcome software that featured a "social interface." They envisioned a package that would employ animated human and animal characters to show users how to go about their computing tasks.

Inside Microsoft, however, employees had immediate concerns about the concept. Software programmers ridiculed the cute characters. Animated characters had been used before only in software for children, making their use in adult environments hard to envision. But Fries and Linnett felt their proposed product had both dynamism and complexity, and they remained convinced that consumers would eagerly buy such programs. They also believed that the home-computer software market—largely untapped at the time and with fewer software standards—would be open to such innovation.

Within the company, Fries had gained quite a bit of relationship credibility. She had started out as a recruiter for the company in 1987 and had worked directly for many of Microsoft's senior executives. They trusted and liked her. In addition, she had been responsible for hiring the company's product and program managers. As a result, she knew all the senior people at Microsoft and had hired many of the people who would be deciding on her product.

Linnett's strength lay in his expertise. In particular, he knew the technology behind an innovative tutorial program called PC Works. In addition, both Fries and Linnett had managed Publisher, a product with a unique help feature called Wizards, which Microsoft's CEO, Bill Gates, had liked. But those factors were sufficient only to get an initial hearing from Microsoft's senior management. To persuade the organization to move forward, the pair would need to improve perceptions of their expertise. It hurt them that this type of social-interface software had no proven track record of success and that they were both novices with such software. Their challenge became one of finding substitutes for their own expertise.

Their first step was a wise one. From within Microsoft, they hired respected technical guru Darrin Massena. With Massena, they developed a set of prototypes to demonstrate that they did indeed understand the software's technology and could make it work. They then tested the prototypes in market research, and users responded enthusiastically. Finally, and most important, they enlisted two Stanford University professors, Clifford Nass and Bryon Reeves, both experts in human-computer interaction. In several meetings with Microsoft senior managers and Gates himself, they presented a rigorously compiled and thorough body of research that demonstrated how and why social-interface software was ideally suited to the average computer user. In addition, Fries and Linnett asserted that considerable jumps in computing power would make more realistic cartoon characters an increasingly malleable technology. Their product, they said, was the leading edge of an incipient software revolution. Convinced, Gates approved a full product-development team, and in January 1995, the product called BOB was launched. BOB went on to sell more than half a million copies, and its concept and technology are being used within Microsoft as a platform for developing several Internet products.

Credibility is the cornerstone of effective persuading; without it, a persuader won't be given the time of day. In the best-case scenario, people enter into a persuasion situation with some measure of expertise and relationship credibility. But it is important to note that credibility along either lines can be built or bought. Indeed, it must be, or the next steps are an exercise in futility.

Frame for common ground

Even if your credibility is high, your position must still appeal strongly to the people you are trying to persuade. After all, few people will jump on board a train that will bring them to ruin or even mild discomfort. Effective persuaders must be adept at describing their positions in terms that illuminate their advantages. As any parent can tell you, the fastest way to get a child to come along willingly on a trip to the grocery store is to point out that there are lollipops by the cash register. That is not deception. It is just a persuasive way of framing the benefits of taking such a journey. In work situations, persuasive framing is obviously more complex, but the underlying principle is the same. It is a process of identifying shared benefits.

Monica Ruffo, an account executive for an advertising agency, offers a good example of persuasive framing. Her client, a fast-food chain, was instituting a promotional campaign in Canada; menu items such as a hamburger, fries, and cola were to be bundled together and sold at a low price. The strategy made sense to corporate headquarters. Its research showed that consumers thought the company's products were higher priced than the competition's, and the company was anxious to overcome this perception. The franchisees, on the other hand, were still experiencing strong sales and were far more concerned about the short-term impact that the new, low prices would have on their profit margins.

A less experienced persuader would have attempted to rationalize headquarters' perspective to the franchisees—to convince them of its validity. But Ruffo framed the change in pricing to demonstrate its benefits to the franchisees themselves. The new value campaign, she explained, would actually improve franchisees' profits. To back up this point, she drew on several sources. A pilot project in Tennessee, for instance, had demonstrated that under the new pricing scheme, the sales of french fries and drinks— the two most profitable items on the menu— had markedly increased. In addition, the company had rolled out medium-sized meal packages in 80% of its U.S. outlets, and franchisees' sales of fries and drinks had jumped 26%. Citing research from a respected business periodical, Ruffo also showed that when customers raised their estimate of the value they receive from a retail establishment by

10%, the establishment's sales rose by 1%. She had estimated that the new meal plan would increase value perceptions by 100%, with the result that franchisee sales could be expected to grow 10%.

Ruffo closed her presentation with a letter written many years before by the company's founder to the organization. It was an emotional letter extolling the values of the company and stressing the importance of the franchisees to the company's success. It also highlighted the importance of the company's position as the low-price leader in the industry. The beliefs and values contained in the letter had long been etched in the minds of Ruffo's audience. Hearing them again only confirmed the company's concern for the franchisees and the importance of their winning formula. They also won Ruffo a standing ovation. That day, the franchisees voted unanimously to support the new meal-pricing plan.

The Ruffo case illustrates why—in choosing appropriate positioning—it is critical first to identify your objective's tangible benefits to the people you are trying to persuade. Sometimes that is easy. Mutual benefits exist. In other situations, however, no shared advantages are readily apparent—or meaningful. In these cases, effective persuaders adjust their positions. They know it is impossible to engage people and gain commitment to ideas or plans without highlighting the advantages to all the parties involved.

At the heart of framing is a solid understanding of your audience. Even before start-

ing to persuade, the best persuaders we have
encountered closely study the issues that
matter to their colleagues. They use conversations, meetings, and other forms of dialogue to collect essential information. They
are good at listening. They test their ideas
with trusted confidants, and they ask questions of the people they will later be persuading. Those steps help them think through
the arguments, the evidence, and the perspectives they will present. Oftentimes, this
process causes them to alter or compromise
their own plans before they even start persuading. It is through this thoughtful, in-
quisitive approach they develop frames that
appeal to their audience.

Consider the case of a manager who was
in charge of process engineering for a jet

engine manufacturer. He had redesigned the work flow for routine turbine maintenance for airline clients in a manner that would dramatically shorten the turnaround time for servicing. Before presenting his ideas to the company's president, he consulted a good friend in the company, the vice president of engineering, who knew the president well. This conversation revealed that the president's prime concern would not be speed or efficiency but profitability. To get the president's buy-in, the vice president explained, the new system would have to improve the company's profitability in the short run by lowering operating expenses.

At first this information had the manager stumped. He had planned to focus on efficiency and had even intended to request additional funding to make the process work. But his conversation with the vice president sparked him to change his position. Indeed, he went so far as to change the work-flow design itself so that it no longer required new investment but rather drove down costs. He then carefully documented the cost savings and profitability gains that his new plan would produce and presented this revised plan to the president. With his initiative positioned anew, the manager persuaded the president and got the project approved.

Provide evidence

With credibility established and a common frame identified, persuasion becomes a matter of presenting evidence. Ordinary evidence, however, won't do. We have found that the most effective persuaders use language in a particular way. They supplement numerical data with examples, stories, metaphors, and analogies to make their positions come alive. That use of language paints a vivid word picture and, in doing so, lends a compelling and tangible quality to the persuader's point of view.

Think about a typical persuasion situation. The persuader is often advocating a goal, strategy, or initiative with an uncertain outcome. Karen Fries and Barry Linnett, for instance, wanted Microsoft to invest millions of dollars in a software package with chancy technology and unknown market demand.

The team could have supported its case solely with market research, financial projections, and the like. But that would have been a mistake, because research shows that most people perceive such reports as not entirely informative. They are too abstract to be completely meaningful or memorable. In essence, the numbers don't make an emotional impact.

By contrast, stories and vivid language do, particularly when they present comparable situations to the one under discussion. A marketing manager trying to persuade senior executives to invest in a new product, for example, might cite examples of similar investments that paid off handsomely. Indeed, we found that people readily draw lessons from such cases. More important, the research shows that listeners absorb information in proportion to its vividness. Thus it is no wonder that Fries and Linnett hit a home run when they presented their case for BOB with the following analogy:

> Imagine you want to cook dinner and you must first go to the supermarket. You have all the flexibility you want—you can cook anything in the world as long as you know how and have the time and desire to do it. When you arrive at the supermarket, you find all these overstuffed aisles with cryptic single-word headings like "sundries" and "ethnic food" and "condiments." These are the menus on typical computer interfaces. The question is whether salt is under condiments or ethnic food or near the potato chip section. There

are surrounding racks and wall spaces, much as our software interfaces now have support buttons, tool bars, and lines around the perimeters. Now after you have collected everything, you still need to put it all together in the correct order to make a meal. If you're a good cook, your meal will probably be good. If you're a novice, it probably won't be.

We [at Microsoft] have been selling under the supermarket category for years, and we think there is a big opportunity for restaurants. That's what we are trying to do now with BOB: pushing the next step with software that is more like going to a restaurant, so the user doesn't spend all of his time searching for the ingredients. We find and put the ingredients together. You sit down, you get comfortable. We bring you a menu. We do the work, you relax. It's an enjoyable experience. No walking around lost trying to find things, no cooking.

Had Fries and Linnett used a literal description of BOB's advantages, few of their highly computer-literate colleagues at Microsoft would have personally related to the menu-searching frustration that BOB was designed to eliminate. The analogy they selected, however, made BOB's purpose both concrete and memorable.

A master persuader, Mary Kay Ash, the founder of Mary Kay Cosmetics, regularly draws on analogies to illustrate and "sell" the business conduct she values. Consider this speech at the company's annual sales convention:

> Back in the days of the Roman Empire, the legions of the emperor conquered the known world. There was, however, one band of peo-

ple that the Romans never conquered. Those people were the followers of the great teacher from Bethlehem. Historians have long since discovered that one of the reasons for the sturdiness of this folk was their habit of meeting together weekly. They shared their difficulties, and they stood side by side. Does this remind you of something? The way we stand side by side and share our knowledge and difficulties with each other in our weekly unit meetings? I have so often observed when a director or unit member is confronted with a personal problem that the unit stands together in helping that sister in distress. What a wonderful circle of friendships we have. Perhaps it's one of the greatest fringe benefits of our company.

Through her vivid analogy, Ash links collective support in the company to a courageous period in Christian history. In doing so, she accomplishes several objectives. First, she drives home her belief that collective support is crucial to the success of the organization. Most Mary Kay salespeople are independent operators who face the daily challenges of direct selling. An emotional support system of fellow salespeople is essential to ensure that self-esteem and confidence remain intact in the face of rejection. Next she suggests by her analogy that solidarity against the odds is the best way to stymie powerful oppressors—to wit, the competition. Finally, Ash's choice of analogy imbues a sense of a heroic mission to the work of her sales force.

You probably don't need to invoke the analogy of the Christian struggle to support your position, but effective persuaders are not afraid of unleashing the immense power of language. In fact, they use it to their utmost advantage.

Connect emotionally

In the business world, we like to think that our colleagues use reason to make their decisions, yet if we scratch below the surface we will always find emotions at play. Good persuaders are aware of the primacy of emotions and are responsive to them in two important ways. First, they show their own emotional commitment to the position they are advocating. Such expression is a delicate matter. If you act too emotional, people may doubt your clearheadedness. But you must also show that your commitment to a goal is not just in your mind but in your heart and gut as well. Without this demonstration of feeling, people may wonder if you actually believe in the position you're championing.

Perhaps more important, however, is that effective persuaders have a strong and accurate sense of their audience's emotional state, and they adjust the tone of their arguments accordingly. Sometimes that means coming on strong, with forceful points. Other times, a whisper may be all that is required. The idea is that whatever your position, you match your emotional fervor to your audience's ability to receive the message.

Effective persuaders seem to have a second sense about how their colleagues have interpreted past events in the organization and how they will probably interpret a proposal. The best persuaders in our study would usually canvass key individuals who had a good pulse on the mood and emotional expectations of those about to be persuaded. They would ask those individuals how various proposals might affect colleagues on an emotional level—in essence, testing possible reactions. They were also quite effective at gathering information through informal conversations in the hallways or at lunch. In the end, their aim was to ensure that the emotional appeal behind their persuasion matched what their audience was already feeling or expecting.

To illustrate the importance of emotional matchmaking in persuasion, consider this example. The president of an aeronautics manufacturing company strongly believed that the maintenance costs and turnaround time of the company's U.S. and foreign competitors were so much better than his own company's that it stood to lose customers and profits. He wanted to communicate his fear and his urgent desire for change to his senior managers. So one afternoon, he called them into the boardroom. On an overhead screen was the projected image of a smiling man flying an old-fashioned biplane with his scarf blowing in the wind. The right half of the transparency was covered. When everyone was seated, the president explained that he felt as this pilot did, given the company's recent good fortune. The organization, after all, had just finished its most successful year in history. But then with a deep sigh, he announced that his happiness was quickly vanishing. As the president lifted the remaining portion of the sheet, he revealed an image of the pilot flying directly into a wall. The president then faced his audience and in a heavy voice said, "This is what I see happening to us." He asserted that the company was headed for a crash if people didn't take action fast. He then went on to lecture the group about the steps needed to counter this threat.

The reaction from the group was immediate and negative. Directly after the meeting, managers gathered in small clusters in the hallways to talk about the president's "scare tactics." They resented what they perceived to be the president's overstatement of the case. As the managers saw it, they had exerted enormous effort that year to break the company's records in sales and profitability. They were proud of their achievements. In fact, they had entered the meeting expecting it would be the moment of recognition. But to their absolute surprise, they were scolded.

The president's mistake? First, he should have canvassed a few members of his senior team to ascertain the emotional state of the group. From that, he would have learned that they were in need of thanks and recognition. He should then have held a separate session devoted simply to praising the team's accomplishments. Later, in a second meeting, he could have expressed his own anxieties about the coming year. And rather than blame the team for ignoring the future, he could have calmly described what he saw as emerging threats to the company and then asked his management team to help him develop new initiatives.

Now let us look at someone who found the right emotional match with his audience: Robert Marcell, head of Chrysler's small-car design team. In the early 1990s, Chrysler was eager to produce a new subcompact— indeed, the company had not introduced a new model of this type since 1978. But senior managers at Chrysler did not want to go it alone. They thought an alliance with a foreign manufacturer would improve the car's design and protect Chrysler's cash stores.

Marcell was convinced otherwise. He believed that the company should bring the design and production of a new subcompact in-house. He knew that persuading senior managers would be difficult, but he also had his own team to contend with. Team members had lost their confidence that they would ever again have the opportunity to create a good car. They were also angry that the United States had once again given up its position to foreign competitors when it came to small cars.

Marcell decided that his persuasion tactics had to be built around emotional themes that would touch his audience. From innumerable conversations around the company, he learned that many people felt as he did—

that to surrender the subcompact's design to a foreign manufacturer was to surrender the company's soul and, ultimately, its ability to provide jobs. In addition, he felt deeply that his organization was a talented group hungry for a challenge and an opportunity to restore its self-esteem and pride. He would need to demonstrate his faith in the team's abilities.

Marcell prepared a 15-minute talk built around slides of his hometown, Iron River, a now defunct mining town in Upper Michigan, devastated, in large part, by foreign mining companies. On the screen flashed recent photographs he had taken of his boarded-up high school, the shuttered homes of his childhood friends, the crumbling ruins of the town's ironworks, closed churches, and an abandoned railroad yard. After a description of each of these places, he said the phrase, "We couldn't compete"—like the refrain of a hymn. Marcell's point was that the same outcome awaited Detroit if the production of small cars was not brought back to the United States. Surrender was the enemy, he said, and devastation would follow if the group did not take immediate action.

Marcell ended his slide show on a hopeful note. He spoke of his pride in his design group and then challenged the team to build a "made-in-America" subcompact that would prove that the United States could still compete. The speech, which echoed the exact sentiments of the audience, rekindled the group's fighting spirit. Shortly after the speech, group members began drafting their ideas for a new car.

Marcell then took his slide show to the company's senior management and ultimately to Chrysler chairman Lee Iacocca. As Marcell showed his slides, he could see that Iacocca was touched. Iacocca, after all, was a fighter and a strongly patriotic man himself. In fact, Marcell's approach was not too different from Iacocca's earlier appeal to the United States Congress to save Chrysler. At the end of the show, Marcell stopped and said, "If we dare to be different, we could be the reason the U.S. auto industry survives. We could be the reason our kids and grandkids don't end up working at fast-food chains." Iacocca stayed on for two hours as Marcell explained in greater detail what his team was planning. Afterward, Iacocca changed his mind and gave Marcell's group approval to develop a car, the Neon.

With both groups, Marcell skillfully matched his emotional tenor to that of the group he was addressing. The ideas he conveyed resonated deeply with his largely Midwestern audience. And rather than leave them in a depressed state, he offered them hope, which was more persuasive than promising doom. Again, this played to the strong patriotic sentiments of his American-heartland audience.

No effort to persuade can succeed without emotion, but showing too much emotion can be as unproductive as showing too little. The important point to remember is that you must match your emotions to your audience's.

THE FORCE OF PERSUASION

The concept of persuasion, like that of power, often confuses and even mystifies businesspeople. It is so complex—and so dangerous when mishandled—that many would rather just avoid it altogether. But like power, persuasion can be a force for enormous good in an organization. It can pull people together, move ideas forward, galvanize change, and forge constructive solutions. To do all that, however, people must understand persuasion for what it is—not convincing and selling but learning and negotiating. Furthermore, it must be seen as an art form that requires commitment and practice, especially as today's business contingencies make persuasion more necessary than ever.

Twelve Years of Watching and Listening

The ideas behind this article spring from three streams of research.

For the last 12 years as both an academic and as a consultant, I have been studying 23 senior business leaders who have shown themselves to be effective change agents. Specifically, I have investigated how these individuals use language to motivate their employees, articulate vision and strategy, and mobilize their organizations to adapt to challenging business environments.

The Necessary Art of Persuasion

Four years ago, I started a second stream of research exploring the capabilities and characteristics of successful cross-functional team leaders. The core of my database comprised interviews with and observations of 18 individuals working in a range of U.S. and Canadian companies. These were not senior leaders as in my earlier studies but low- and middle-level managers. Along with interviewing the colleagues of these people, I also compared their skills with those of other team leaders—in particular, with the leaders of less successful cross-functional teams engaged in similar initiatives within the same companies. Again, my focus was on language, but I also studied the influence of interpersonal skills.

The similarities in the persuasion skills possessed by both the change-agent leaders and effective team leaders prompted me to explore the academic literature on persuasion and rhetoric, as well as on the art of gospel preaching. Meanwhile, to learn how most managers approach the persuasion process, I observed several dozen managers in company meetings, and I employed simulations in company executive-education programs where groups of managers had to persuade one another on hypothetical business objectives. Finally, I selected a group of 14 managers known for their outstanding abilities in constructive persuasion. For several months, I interviewed them and their colleagues and observed them in actual work situations.

Four Ways Not to Persuade

In my work with managers as a researcher and as a consultant, I have had the unfortunate opportunity to see executives fail miserably at persuasion. Here are the four most common mistakes people make:

1. *They attempt to make their case with an up-front, hard sell.* I call this the John Wayne approach. Managers strongly state their position at the outset, and then through a process of persistence, logic, and exuberance, they try to push the idea to a close. In reality, setting out a strong position at the start of a persuasion effort gives potential opponents something to grab onto—and fight against. It's far better to present your position with the finesse and reserve of a lion tamer, who engages his "partner" by showing him the legs of a chair. In other words, effective persuaders don't begin the process by giving their colleagues a clear target in which to set their jaws.

2. *They resist compromise.* Too many managers see compromise as surrender, but it is essential to constructive persuasion. Before people buy into a proposal, they want to see

that the persuader is flexible enough to respond to their concerns. Compromises can often lead to better, more sustainable shared solutions.

By not compromising, ineffective persuaders unconsciously send the message that they think persuasion is a one-way street. But persuasion is a process of give-and-take. Kathleen Reardon, a professor of organizational behavior at the University of Southern California, points out that a persuader rarely changes another person's behavior or viewpoint without altering his or her own in the process. To persuade meaningfully, we must not only listen to others but also incorporate their perspectives into our own.

3. *They think the secret of persuasion lies in presenting great arguments.* In persuading people to change their minds, great arguments matter. No doubt about it. But argu-

ments, per se, are only one part of the equa-
tion. Other factors matter just as much, such
as the persuader's credibility and his or her
ability to create a proper, mutually beneficial
frame for a position, connect on the right
emotional level with an audience, and communicate through vivid language that makes
arguments come alive.

4. *They assume persuasion is a one-shot effort.*
   Persuasion is a process, not an event.
   Rarely, if ever, is it possible to arrive at a
   shared solution on the first try. More often
   than not, persuasion involves listening to
   people, testing a position, developing a new
   position that reflects input from the group,
   more testing, incorporating compromises,
   and then trying again. If this sounds like a
   slow and difficult process, that's because it
   is. But the results are worth the effort.

ABOUT THE AUTHOR

At the time of this article, *Jay A. Conger* was
a professor of organizational behavior at the
University of Southern California's Marshall
School of Business in Los Angeles, where
he directed the Leadership Institute. He is
currently the Henry Kravis Research Chair
Professor of Leadership at Claremont
McKenna College.

ALSO BY THIS AUTHOR

***Harvard Business Review* Articles**

"Make Your Company a Talent Factory"
with Douglas A. Ready

"Developing Your Leadership Pipeline"
with Robert M. Fulmer

"Appraising Boardroom Performance"
with David Finegold and Edward E. Lawler III

.

Harvard Business Review Case Study

"Orit Gadiesh: Pride at Bain & Co."
with Nancy Rothbard

Article Summary

The Idea in Brief

Today, employees don't just ask, "What should I do?" They also ask, "*Why* should I do it?" This is where persuasion comes into play. It's often perceived as a skill only for sales and deal closing- just another form of manipulation. But persuasion is much more than a selling technique, and it represents the opposite of deception. Effective persuasion is a learning and negotiating process for leading your colleagues to a *shared solution* to a problem.

The Idea at Work

The process of persuasion has four steps:

1. *Establish credibility.* Your credibility grows out of two sources: expertise and relationships. If you have a history of well-informed, sound judgment, your colleagues will trust your expertise. If you've demonstrated that you can work in the best interest of others, your colleagues will have confidence in your relationships.

   If you are weak on the expertise side, bolster your position by

   - learning more through formal and informal education-for example, conversations with in-house experts

   - hiring recognized outside experts

   - launching pilot projects.

To fill in the relationship gap, try

- meeting one-on-one with key people

- involving like-minded coworkers who have good support with your audience.

Example: Two developers at Microsoft envisioned a controversial new software product, but both were technology novices. By working closely with technical experts and market testing a prototype, they persuaded management that the new product was ideally suited to the average computer user. It sold half a million units.

2. *Frame goals on common ground.* Tangibly describe the benefits of your position. The fastest way to get a child to the grocery store is to point out the lollipops by the cash register. That is not deception—it's persuasion.

When no shared advantages are apparent, adjust your position.

Example: An ad agency executive persuaded skeptical fast-food franchisees to support headquarters' new price discounts. She cited reliable research showing how the pricing scheme improved franchisees' profits. They supported the new plan unanimously.

3. *Vividly reinforce your position.* Ordinary evidence won't do. Make numerical data more compelling with examples, stories, and metaphors that have an emotional impact.

Example: The founder of Mary Kay Cosmetics made a speech comparing salespeople's weekly meetings to gatherings among Christians resisting Roman rule. This drove home the importance of a mutually supportive sales force and imbued the work with a sense of heroic mission.

4. *Connect emotionally.* Adjust your own emotional tone to match each audience's ability to receive your message. Learn how your colleagues have interpreted past events in the organization and sense how they will probably interpret your proposal. Test key individuals' possible reactions.

Example: A Chrysler team leader raised the morale of employees demoralized by foreign competition and persuaded management to bring a new car design in-house. He showed both audiences slides of his hometown, which had been devastated by foreign mining competition. His patriotic appeal reinvigorated his team, and the chairman approved the plan.